SPACECRAFT TECHNOLOGY

John Mason

The Bookwright Press
New York · 1990

Titles in this series

Aircraft Technology

Car Technology

Spacecraft Technology

TV and Video Technology

Ship Technology

Train Technology

First published in the
United States in 1990 by
The Bookwright Press
387 Park Avenue South
New York, NY 10016

First published in 1989
Wayland (Publishers) Ltd
61 Western Road, Hove
East Sussex BN3 1JD, England

Library of Congress Cataloging-in-Publication Data
Mason, John (John W.)
      Spacecraft technology/by John Mason.
          p.   cm.—(Technology in action).
      Includes bibliographical references.
      Summary: An introduction to space technology,
discussing the principles of rockets, various types of
satellites, travel in the solar system, and space stations.
      ISBN 0-531-18328-9
      1. Astronautics—Juvenile literature. [1. Astronautics.]
I. Title. II. Series.
TL793.M36 1990   2. Space vehicles
629.4 — dc20   89-17700
              C   629.47   CIP
                                                   AC

Typeset by Direct Image Photosetting Limited, Sussex, England
Printed in Italy by G. Canale & C.S.p.A., Turin

Front cover An artist's impression of what a future military satellite
might look like when positioned in orbit above the Earth.

Contents

1 ▷ Into space

At the beginning of the twentieth century, new technologies were being developed, and cars were beginning to appear on the roads. In December 1903, two American brothers, Orville and Wilbur Wright, made the first powered flight in their *Wright Flyer 1*. At that time few believed that aircraft would soon become so important or that travel in space would ever become a possibility, although a French writer, Jules Verne, had written a prophetic book about space in 1865. He imagined people going into space by being fired like a bullet from a huge gun.

In Verne's story, *From the Earth to the Moon*, a gun was pointed toward the sky, and three space travelers were blasted away from Earth at tremendous speed. They sped to the Moon in a spacecraft shaped like a cone. When they returned to Earth, they splashed down in the sea and were picked up quite unharmed. About 100 years later, on July 21, 1969, two astronauts made the first landing on the Moon's rocky surface.

On the Earth's surface we are protected from the harsh environment of outer space by the thin protective blanket of air that we call the atmosphere. The air that we breathe is invisible, and it becomes thinner and thinner and more difficult to breathe as we rise higher away from the Earth's surface. Eventually there is no air at all and we reach empty space. Because there is no air of any kind in space, we call it a vacuum, which means empty space. For this and other reasons the exploration of space, either by manned or unmanned spacecraft, requires special technologies.

These technologies are very costly, and many people find it difficult to understand how such vast expenditure can be justified. Although, at present, a large part of space exploration appears to be for military purposes and is seen as a contest between the United States and the USSR, there have been many other benefits. The need to miniaturize the instruments used in spacecraft led to the development of

Left Two American brothers, Orville and Wilbur Wright, were the first men to fly successfully in a powered airplane. Their first powered flight in the *Wright Flyer 1* took place on December 17, 1903.

In this artist's impression, the American probe Magellan, named after the sixteenth-century explorer Ferdinand Magellan, is shown in orbit around Venus, mapping the surface of the planet.

numerous technologies, including the microprocessor, which have since found use in our everyday lives. Communications satellites help ships and aircraft to navigate, and relay television programs and telephone messages around the world. Satellites, that take photographs from space, tell us more about our own planet and help in forecasting the weather.

Most important, spacecraft are beginning to tell us more than we have ever known before about the vast universe of which our small planet is a part.

Finally, it is human nature to want to explore the unknown and to make new discoveries. This is probably the main reason why people want to travel in space.

If you throw a ball up into the air, it reaches a certain height and then falls back down to Earth again. It is pulled downward by the force of gravity, the same force that keeps our feet firmly on the ground. The Earth, the Moon, the Sun and all the stars in the universe have their own gravity. If you throw the ball a little harder, it will rise to a greater height before falling back again. If you could throw the ball into the air at a speed of 25,000 mph (40,000 kph) it would never fall down to Earth again. The Earth's gravity would not be strong enough to pull it back. The ball would escape into space. This speed is called the Earth's escape velocity. A spacecraft has to travel upward at this speed to escape into space.

Jules Verne was wrong. The space vehicles of today are not fired from a huge gun. The sudden jolt of the gun firing would kill any people on board. Some other means had to be found to overcome the pull of the Earth's gravity. Balloons and aircraft work only when they are surrounded by air. They need air to support them and give them lift. The engines of aircraft need air to make them work, so they would be of no use in space where there is no air.

In 1895, a shy, deaf Russian teacher called Konstantin Tsiolkovskii found the answer to this problem. He suggested the use of rockets. Tsiolkovskii did not build a rocket himself, and at the time nobody took much interest. It was

Below Dr. Robert H. Goddard (second from right) and his assistants placing the rocket in the launch tower. The test firing took place October 27, 1931 in a prairie 12 mi (20 km) northwest of Roswell, New Mexico.

American astronaut Bruce McCandless becomes a human "satellite" as he makes the first untethered spacewalk during a test of the gas-propelled manned maneuvering unit in February 1984. He moved to a distance of over 300 feet from the Shuttle.

not until 1926 that an American, Robert Goddard, launched the first successful liquid-fueled rockets. His first rocket traveled at no more than 62 mph (100 kph) and stayed aloft for only a few seconds.

Rocket research was also carried out in Germany before World War II by scientists such as Werner von Braun. They developed the first effective high-altitude rockets. These were the powerful V2 weapons, used against England in the final stages of the war. After the war, many of the German team went to the United States to continue their research. From their work the first rockets were developed for space flight.

The rocket carrying a spacecraft starts slowly and builds up speed until escape velocity is reached. A rocket works in space because it does not have to be surrounded by air for it to move. It works on the principle of reaction. An ordinary fireworks rocket consists of a hollow tube filled with gunpowder, closed at one end. When the gunpowder is lit, it burns very quickly. This makes a huge quantity of hot gas, which rushes out of the open end of the rocket. The action of the gas going one way thrusts the nose of the rocket the other way. The gunpowder provides the power to make the rocket rise upward. Gunpowder is solid fuel, and a firework rocket is a solid-fueled rocket. When gunpowder burns out, a rocket falls back to Earth. Gunpowder cannot be used as fuel for a space rocket because it burns too quickly.

Below First tested on May 15, 1987, the Soviet Energia rocket is the world's most powerful launch vehicle. It consists of a central core 197 ft (60 m) tall, surrounded by pairs of strap-on booster rockets, each 130 ft (40 m) tall. These can be re-used. With four strap-on boosters it can lift 170 tons into orbit.

Most rockets use liquid fuels. Two of these liquids, such as hydrogen and oxygen, are carried in separate tanks. They are pumped through pipes into a chamber, and when they mix, they react very violently. This produces enormous quantities of hot gases, which rush out of the nozzle at the base of the rocket propelling it upward. Liquid fuels continue to burn at a steady rate for far longer than solid fuels, so they produce more thrust. Liquid-fueled rockets are also safer than solid-fueled ones. Once lit, a solid-fueled rocket will burn until all the fuel is exhausted. In a liquid-fueled rocket, the mixing of the two liquid fuels can be easily and therefore more safely controlled.

The thrust from one rocket is not enough to reach escape velocity. This problem is solved by using two or more rockets, one on top of the other. This is called a multi-stage rocket. The huge first stage provides the initial thrust to lift the whole rocket from the ground. When its fuel is used up, this stage is jettisoned and drops away. In this way the rocket does not have to carry unnecessary weight. The next stage takes over and provides the thrust to take the rest of the rocket into space. Three stages were used for the giant American Saturn V rocket used to launch astronauts to the Moon. The Russians have adopted a rather different approach. They use a central basic rocket with pairs of strap-on boosters at the side.

Right Standing over 360 ft (110 m) tall, the giant three-stage Saturn V rocket was the largest and most powerful U.S. launch vehicle ever built. It was developed for the Apollo project and was capable of sending about 50 tons of payload into orbit around the Moon. The first-stage motors produced 3,470 tons of thrust at liftoff.

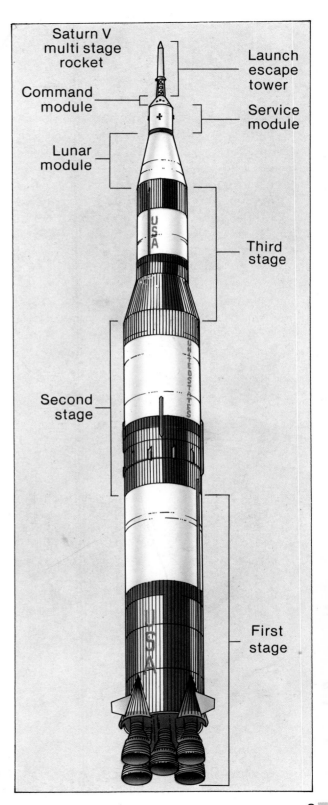

Saturn V multi stage rocket

Launch escape tower

Command module

Service module

Lunar module

Third stage

Second stage

First stage

The Moon orbits around the Earth and is our only natural satellite. Nowadays the Earth is surrounded by several hundred working artificial satellites as well. Each of these circles our planet, moving along an orbit well over one hundred miles above the ground. To launch a satellite into orbit around the Earth, it is not necessary to achieve escape velocity. A low orbit can be achieved by a satellite when released from a rocket traveling at 15,500 mph (25,000 kph).

The satellites orbiting the Earth have many different jobs. Some jobs need more than one satellite to carry them out. Long-distance communications are carried out by a network of

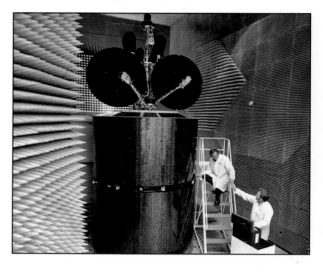

Below Diagram showing the components of an Intelsat 4A communications spacecraft.

Above Engineers inspect an Intelsat 4 communications satellite.

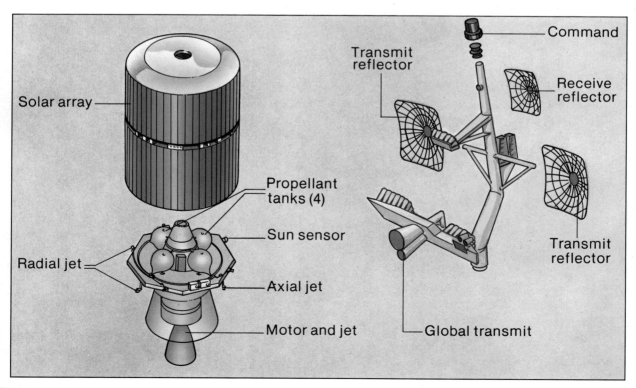

Solar array

Propellant tanks (4)

Sun sensor

Radial jet

Axial jet

Motor and jet

Transmit reflector

Command

Receive reflector

Transmit reflector

Global transmit

Above Telstar 1, launched in July 1962, was the world's first commercial satellite.

satellites that receive radio signals from ground stations around the world and relay them to other ground stations far away, possibly in another continent.

The use of satellites for communications was first suggested by the science fiction writer Arthur C. Clarke in 1945. He predicted that if a satellite was put into the correct orbit around the Earth, at a height of 22,300 mi (35,900 km) above the equator, it would move eastward at the same speed as the Earth spins. It would then "hover" above any point on the equator. This is called a geostationary orbit. Many communications satellites have geostationary orbits, but some, such as the Russian Molniya series, have very eccentric orbits. They travel along a long, narrow oval path that swings low on one side of the Earth but high on the other.

From orbit, a communications satellite can relay telephone, telex and television signals across the world at the speed of light. Signals are beamed to the satellite from large saucer-shaped antennas about 100 ft (30m) across on the ground. When a signal reaches the satellite, it is very faint. So instruments on the satellite amplify the signal before sending it back down to another receiving dish elsewhere on Earth. They also change the signal so that it does not interfere with the incoming one.

As well as for peaceful uses, satellites are also used to spy on other countries. They can "listen in" to radio messages from thousands of sources across the world. They observe the movements of troops, track ships across the oceans, and submarines beneath the surface. Many spy satellites take photographs from space of military bases and missile launching sites. Their cameras are so powerful that they would be able to "see" a person on the ground from a height of 62 mi (100 km).

In the mid-1960s, it was realized that there was a need to obtain accurate information on the world's shrinking natural resources – forests, minerals and fossil fuels such as coal and oil. A series of Earth resources satellites was developed. These satellites orbit the Earth scanning its surface continuously using high quality cameras. Their pictures help to make maps, monitor the growth and health of forests and crops, look at areas of flooding or drought and locate forest fires. They also show pollution in the atmosphere or oceans and plot the movements of icebergs.

Knowledge of the weather and the accuracy of weather forecasts has greatly improved with the use of weather satellites. They measure wind speeds at sea level and higher in the atmosphere. They observe the height of ocean waves and the distance between them. They photograph the constantly changing cloud patterns, and watch the weather on a worldwide scale. Most important, they can track devastating tropical storms. An early warning to areas where such storms may pass can save lives.

The cameras aboard these satellites use a process called remote sensing. They view the

Above The equipment used on the Landsat D satellite for mapping the Earth's surface. **Below** Diagram showing how the Earth's surface is mapped in a series of overlapping strips, each image consisting of a number of picture elements or pixels.

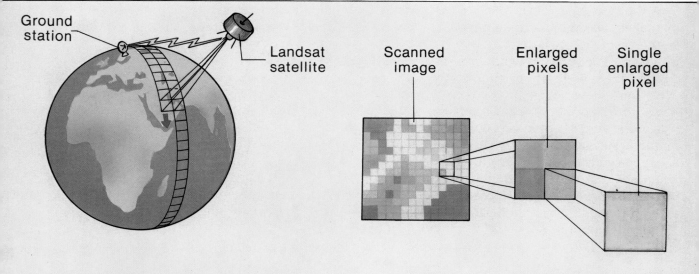

Ground station

Landsat satellite

Scanned image

Enlarged pixels

Single enlarged pixel

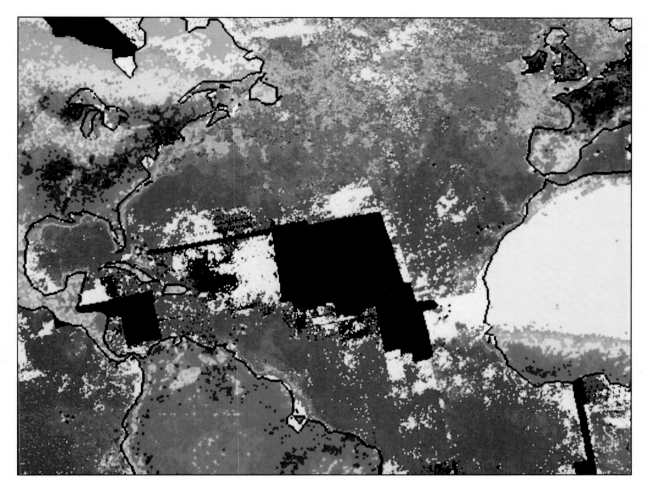

NASA's coastal zone color scanner operating on board the Nimbus 7 satellite obtained this picture of the entire North Atlantic Ocean. It shows the distribution of microscopic plant life or plankton in the surface waters.

Earth in both visible light, which can be seen by the human eye, and in invisible infrared light, which is sometimes called heat or thermal radiation. The infrared pictures are very useful. Warm areas of land or sea appear dark, and cold areas look bright. High cloud, which is very cold, appears white, and lower levels of cloud appear in various shades of gray, depending on their height and temperature. Healthy plants appear dark red on color infrared pictures because they strongly reflect infrared light. Plants affected by disease and drought can be identified by the different colors they reflect.

Most satellites studying the Earth from space orbit in a north-south direction. They circle the Earth passing over both poles, while the Earth spins beneath them. On each orbit the cameras on board cover a narrow strip all around the Earth. This strip may be only 125 mi (200 km) wide in the case of the Earth resources satellites, but over 1,900 mi (3,000 km) wide for the weather satellites. The strip consists of a sequence of pictures, taken one after the other, with some overlap between them. The whole of the Earth's surface is scanned twice each day. A few weather satellites have geostationary orbits, and can photograph a complete hemisphere of the Earth at a time.

The Earth's atmosphere makes it difficult for astronomers to study the universe. Apart from clouds, even on a clear night the air itself blocks out most of the radiation from space. (Visible light is only a very small part of this radiation.) In addition, the atmosphere distorts what little radiation does reach the ground. To observe the X-rays, ultraviolet (UV) and much of the infrared radiation coming from objects in space, astronomers put their specialized instruments on satellites above the atmosphere.

The first X-ray satellite was Uhuru, launched in December 1970. It provided the first detailed X-ray map of the sky and identified over 330 X-ray sources. Since then, there have been various other X-ray satellites. One was Ariel 5, which proved to be extremely successful. Then came the Einstein and EXOSAT satellites with their X-ray telescopes.

X-rays can be reflected only if they strike a polished metal surface at a very shallow angle, rather like a flat stone bouncing off the surface

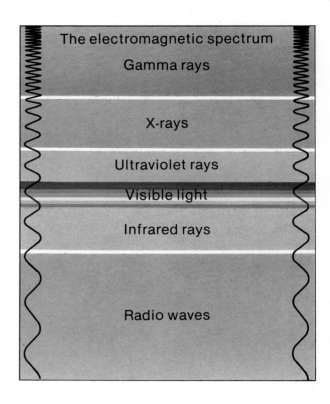

The electromagnetic spectrum

Gamma rays

X-rays

Ultraviolet rays

Visible light

Infrared rays

Radio waves

Below An X-ray picture, taken by the satellite HEAO-2, of the Crab Nebula, the remnant of a star that was seen to explode in AD 1054. The bright object at the center is a pulsating star called a pulsar.

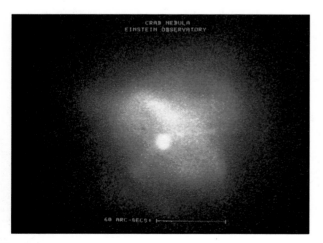

Above This diagram shows the entire electromagnetic spectrum. This consists of a number of bands of radiation, each having a different wavelength. Of these, visible light, which our eyes can see, is only a small part. Visible light consists of a series of waves, with each color having a different wavelength. Visible light can be split up into seven colors – red, orange, yellow, green, blue, indigo and violet. These colors are known as the visible spectrum and together make up white light. Beyond violet, there are invisible rays such as ultraviolet and X-rays, with shorter wavelengths. Beyond red, there are longer wavelength invisible rays such as infrared and radio waves. Objects in outer space give off rays of varying wavelengths. These can be detected by "telescopes" carried on spacecraft in Earth orbit above the layers of the atmosphere.

of a pond. The telescopes therefore look like a bottomless metal bucket with a highly polished interior. Recently the Russian Kvant module on the Mir space station and the Japanese Ginga satellite have made a number of important X-ray observations.

Ultraviolet observations from space began with the Copernicus satellite in 1972. The International Ultraviolet Explorer (IUE), launched in January 1978, has been one of the most successful satellites ever built. It has made thousands of important observations over the past eleven years. It carries an 18-in (45-cm) aperture UV telescope and two television cameras.

Infrared studies began with the highly successful InfraRed Astronomical Satellite (IRAS) in 1983. It carried a 24-in (60-cm) telescope and very sensitive detectors. The whole tele-scope had to be cooled to below minus 500°F (-260°C) to eliminate heat coming from the satellite itself. Liquid helium was used to cool it, but the supply was gradually used up and after three hundred days the instruments ceased to function. IRAS made many exciting discoveries and a catalogue of over 240,000 infrared sources in space was produced.

The most exciting development in astronomy from space is the Hubble Space Telescope (HST). Launched by the U.S. Space Shuttle, it will be free from the effects of the atmosphere. The HST will produce sharper images than ever before. It should be able to detect objects fifty times fainter and seven times farther away than can at present be seen from the ground. The HST will lead to a vast increase in our knowledge of the universe.

THE HUBBLE SPACE TELESCOPE
1. Movable protective cover
2. Solar panel to provide electrical power
3. Main mirror 7.9 ft (2.4 m) in diameter
4. Scientific instrument module
5. Fine guidance sensor
6. Secondary mirror assembly
7. Dish antenna

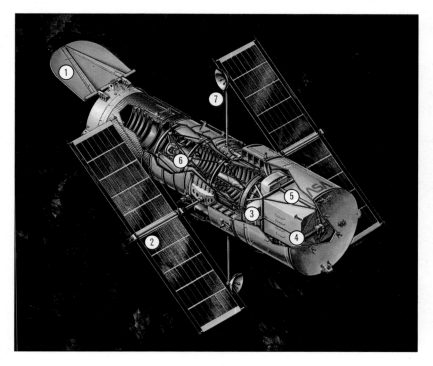

Left The Hubble Space Telescope (HST), due for launch from the cargo-bay of the U.S. Space Shuttle early in 1990, will give astronomers the clearest view of the universe yet. Orbiting high above the Earth's turbulent atmosphere, the main mirror of the HST will collect light from objects in space, producing sharper, more detailed pictures than ever before possible. The images formed by the telescope will be converted into electronic signals and beamed down to Earth by satellite. Scientists will use computers to convert the signals into pictures.

Astronomers and scientists need to learn all they can about our neighbors in space, the Moon, the Sun and the nearest planets. To do this they have developed spacecraft called interplanetary probes.

In January 1959, the Russian probe Luna 1 passed within 3,728 mi (6,000 km) of the Moon, our closest neighbor. This type of flight is called a fly-by probe. The first close-up pictures of the Moon were taken by three unmanned American spacecraft, Rangers 7, 8 and 9, in 1964 and 1965, as they were crashed onto the surface. Later, five Lunar Orbiters circled the Moon several thousand times, taking high quality pictures for the first photographic lunar atlas.

The first successful soft-lander probe was Luna 9 in February 1966. As gravity pulled the spacecraft toward the Moon, retro-rockets were fired toward the surface. These slowed the spacecraft down so that it landed gently without damage.

After the United States successfully put men on the Moon, the Russians went a step further. They soft-landed the unmanned probe Luna 16 on the Moon in September 1970. It scooped up a little lunar soil, blasted off again, and brought it back to Earth. This is called a sample-return probe.

Below After landing on the surface of Mars in a region known as Utopia, the cameras on the Viking Lander 2 spacecraft sent back many pictures of the reddish landscape.

Left Eighteen months after the first men landed on the Moon, the USSR launched Luna 17. It carried the first unmanned lunar roving vehicle, called Lunokhod 1. This picture shows a prototype being tested on Earth. It resembled a saucepan on wheels. There were eight wheels altogether, and a team of drivers on Earth could control it. Lunokhod 1 operated for eleven months after its arrival on the Moon in November 1970, climbing slopes and weaving in and out of craters.

Soviet and U.S. probes have also explored the nearest planets to the Earth – Mercury and Venus, which are closer to the Sun than we are, and Mars, which is farther away. Mariner 10 flew by Mercury three times in 1974 and 1975, showing a cratered surface similar to that of the Moon. It also took pictures of Venus, but the surface of Venus is always hidden by a dense, poisonous atmosphere. The Russians success-fully landed several of their Venera probes on its surface. Other spacecraft circled Venus, sending back information by radio.

Mars has been visited by many space probes since Mariner 4 flew by the planet in July 1965. Many of the Soviet Mars probes failed before sending back any information, but the U.S. probes have had better luck. Mariner 9 went into orbit around Mars in November 1971. It took pictures showing the polar ice-caps, huge volcanoes, vast canyons and features like dried-up river beds. In 1975, two American Viking spacecraft were launched on a mission to search for life on Mars. On arrival, each probe split into two parts. The orbiters photographed the surface, and observed clouds and weather patterns. The landers touched down on the Martian surface. They sent back pictures of the red desertlike terrain covered with small rocks. They scooped up soil and analyzed it, but the tests for life were inconclusive.

Above As the American probe Mariner 10 approached Mercury on March 29, 1974, it took a series of photographs that were fitted together like a mosaic to produce this view of the planet. The probe was about 124,000 mi (200,000 km) from Mercury. A large number of craters were discovered, some over 120 mi (193 km) in diameter.

17

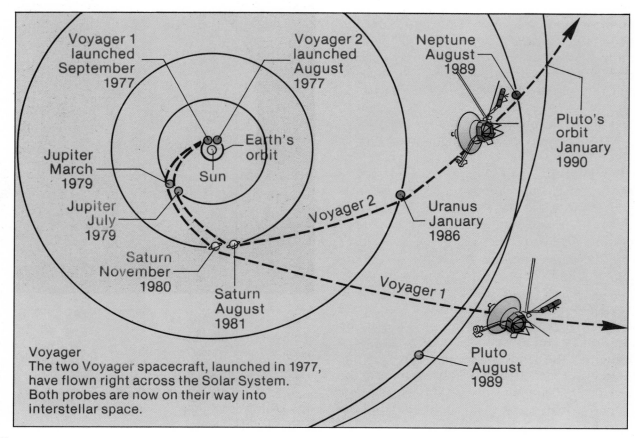

8 — Across the Solar System

Four U.S. robot space probes have also been despatched to take a close-up look at the more distant and largest members of the Sun's family. Traveling beyond the orbit of Mars, it is necessary to cross a region where several thousand tiny, irregularly shaped pieces of rock, known as asteroids, circle the Sun. The largest is only 620 mi (1,000 km) across. The probes Pioneers 10 and 11, launched in March 1972 and April 1973, proved that it was possible to travel safely through the asteroid belt to the giant planets beyond. They both flew by Jupiter, and Pioneer 11 also flew past Saturn and photographed its magnificent rings.

The highly successful Voyager spacecraft, launched in 1977, have also carried out long-distance voyages across interplanetary space. They took advantage of an alignment of the outer planets that happens only once every 175 years. Between 1979 and 1989 Jupiter, Saturn, Uranus and Neptune lined up on the same side of the Sun. So Voyager could use the gravity of one planet to swing it onto the next in line, passing by each giant planet in turn. Both Voyagers 1 and 2 went to Jupiter and Saturn. They sent back thousands of high quality photographs of these giant planets, and of their many moons and ring systems. Voyager 1 took a close-up look at Saturn's fascinating moon, Titan, and then headed out of the Solar System.

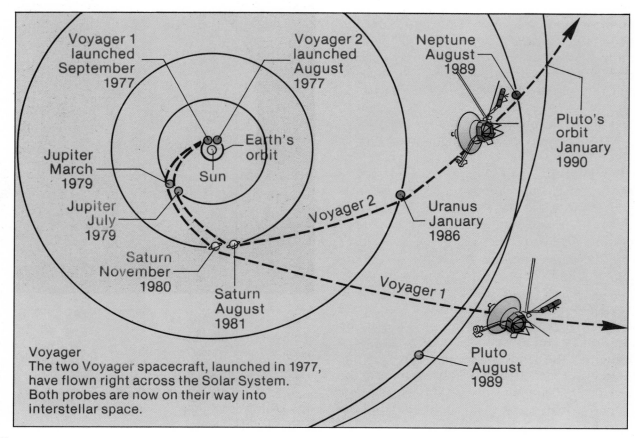

Voyager 1 launched September 1977 — Voyager 2 launched August 1977 — Neptune August 1989 — Pluto's orbit January 1990 — Jupiter March 1979 — Jupiter July 1979 — Earth's orbit — Sun — Voyager 2 — Uranus January 1986 — Saturn November 1980 — Saturn August 1981 — Voyager 1 — Pluto August 1989

Voyager
The two Voyager spacecraft, launched in 1977, have flown right across the Solar System. Both probes are now on their way into interstellar space.

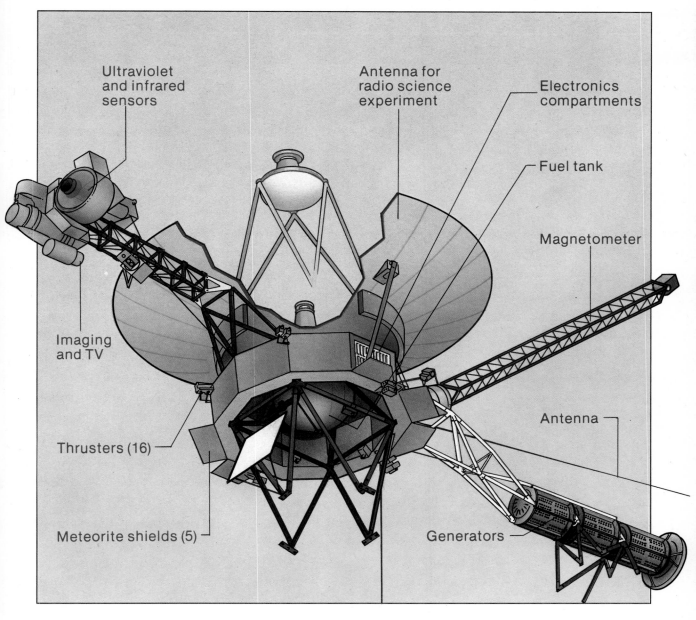

Ultraviolet and infrared sensors

Antenna for radio science experiment

Electronics compartments

Fuel tank

Magnetometer

Imaging and TV

Thrusters (16)

Antenna

Meteorite shields (5)

Generators

Above The various parts that make up the American Voyager spacecraft.

Voyager 2 continued onward, flying by Uranus in January 1986. It passed Neptune in August 1989. By the end of these missions, only tiny Pluto of the planets will remain unexplored at close range. However, that may not be the end of the story. Pluto is much smaller than anyone expected, and some astronomers believe that there is yet another planet beyond it. They will be tracking the Pioneer and Voyager spacecraft very precisely to see if they are being pulled off course by an unknown planet.

Eventually all the Pioneer and Voyager spacecraft will leave the Solar System altogether, and will enter the space between the stars. After millions of years they may well pass through other star systems.

Some exciting missions are now being planned to take place during the next ten years. The first planetary probe to be launched from the U.S. Space Shuttle, the Magellan Venus radar mapper, is due to begin studies of the planet in 1990. Since the surface of Venus is covered by dense clouds, and cannot be photographed, instruments will be used to map its surface in great detail. Then there is the ambitious Galileo probe. After launch from the Shuttle in October 1989, it began a six-year journey to Jupiter. It will fly past Venus and twice past the Earth as it gathers speed. It will pass two asteroids on the way, reaching Jupiter at the end of 1995. The Galileo probe will then split into two parts. The orbiter will make repeated passes of Jupiter's moons, while a probe parachutes into the planet's dense atmosphere.

The USSR have recently begun a major program of Mars exploration. Probes may be launched at roughly two-year intervals from 1994 until the end of the century. Some will orbit the planet, others will soft-land or drive across the surface. Some may even return samples of Martian soil to Earth. The United States too has Mars as a target. The Mars Observer probe will attempt to produce the most detailed map ever of the Martian surface. The United States has also tested several designs of Mars roving vehicles.

Many other projects are planned, such as the ambitious Cassini mission to Saturn and its largest moon Titan. The United States will provide the orbiting spacecraft. This will make repeated orbits around Saturn, studying its many moons and unique ring system in detail. The European Space Agency will provide the Titan probe, which will parachute into the moon's atmosphere. Cassini is due for launch in 1996.

Probes may also be launched to find out more about the minor members of the Sun's family – the comets and asteroids. These probes will include the U.S. CRAF (Comet Rendezvous and Asteroid Fly-by) mission and the joint European and Soviet Vesta probe to study the third largest

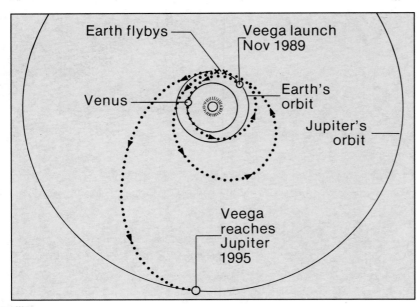

Left After launch from Earth, the American Galileo probe will travel to Jupiter by a very circuitous route. The total journey will take about six years. It will pass Venus once and the Earth twice during the trip, getting a little "kick" from their gravity each time it does so. This is called VEEGA, which stands for Venus Earth Earth Gravity Assist.

Above The American Magellan spacecraft being tested by technicians before launch.

asteroid. The Europeans also plan a Comet Nucleus Sample Return mission in the late 1990s. This would involve sending a spacecraft to intercept the tiny dust-covered ice ball at the heart of a comet. Comets are believed to contain some of the oldest material in our Solar System. A probe would retrieve a sample of the comet's nucleus and return it to Earth for examination.

Whenever astronauts are launched into space, they experience high G-forces. When a car makes a fast start, you feel as if you are being pushed back into your seat. You are thrown forward when the car brakes suddenly unless you are well strapped in. These are examples of G-forces. On Earth, we always feel a force of 1G due to the pull of gravity. To overcome Earth's gravity, a space rocket has to blast off violently, subjecting the astronauts to high G-forces. This is because the only practical way to lift heavy loads into space is to use short bursts of high acceleration. These G-forces make the body feel extremely heavy. Because of this, astronauts are strapped in with a harness that can withstand high G-forces. At one time space scientists thought that high G-forces might cause astronauts to have difficulty seeing or thinking properly. So they had to have special training to familiarize them with the tremendous forces of acceleration and deceleration.

To simulate the speeding up of the rocket at launch and the sudden slowing of the spacecraft on reentering the atmosphere, early astronauts were spun around in a large centrifuge. They were accelerated to enormous speed, until they were pressed back into their couches by a force eighteen times their normal weight – a force of 18G. During early launches in the Mercury one-man and Gemini two-man space missions, astronauts experienced up to 7G at liftoff, and even up to 11G on reentry. Shuttle astronauts do not experience such high G-forces. A force of 3G during the launch is normal. This means that healthy men and women can go into space on the Shuttle with less physical space training.

Once in orbit, the crew of a spacecraft have no feeling of weight. They are weightless. On Earth, you feel weight only because something – the ground you stand on – resists the pull of gravity on your body. When there is no resistance, such

Left In April 1984, during a seven-day flight of the Space Shuttle Challenger, a colony of 3,000 bees traveled in space, enclosed in an aluminum box. A similar group of bees remained on Earth. By observing the two colonies of bees very closely scientists were able to see how the bees in the weightless conditions of space built their honeycombs as compared with the colony on Earth.

Left During the final flight aboard the Skylab space station, U.S. astronauts Edward Gibson and Gerald Carr are seen here demonstrating the effects of Zero-G, or weightlessness, in the forward equipment area. Together with fellow crew member William Pogue, the three men spent 84 days aboard Skylab, the longest U.S. space mission ever undertaken. The Skylab missions helped doctors find out how crews can stay fit and healthy when they live and work in space for long periods.

as when you are falling, you are weightless. Astronauts become weightless as soon as the rocket motors are shut off. No force then resists the pull of gravity. The astronauts and their spacecraft are falling freely together, both weightless. Strange things happen in weightlessness. An object held at arm's length and released will not fall. Weightless liquid will not pour. All objects, unless fixed down, will float around the spacecraft. At one time it was thought that the human body would be unable to adapt to long periods of weightlessness. Many experiments have been carried out to investigate these problems.

In 1961, President John F. Kennedy set American scientists the challenge of landing men on the Moon before 1970. The plan was called the Apollo project. Twelve astronauts were successfully landed on the Moon's surface. It began with Apollo 11 on July 20, 1969, and ended with Apollo 17 in December 1972.

It took a very large, powerful rocket to send three astronauts to the Moon. The giant Saturn V rocket stood over 360 ft (110 m) tall – as high as a 40-story tower block. All that came back to Earth was the tiny cone-shaped Command Module (CM), containing the crew. The Apollo spacecraft was 82 ft (25 m) tall. It consisted of several parts. The Spacecraft Lunar Module Adaptor (SLMA) linked the Apollo spacecraft to the rocket during liftoff. It surrounded and protected the Lunar Module (LM). The CM was attached to the Service Module (SM). Together they were called the CSM. The SM was a cylinder 24.6 ft (7.5 m) across, with its own rocket motor and fuel tanks.

After launch, the Apollo spacecraft and third stage of the rocket entered Earth orbit. Then the motors of the third stage were fired sending the astronauts off to the Moon. The CSM, separated from the SLMA, was turned around and it docked with the LM. The CSM and LM then headed off toward the Moon. Once in lunar orbit, one astronaut remained in the CSM, while the other two entered the LM for the descent to the Moon. There were two parts to the LM, called the descent stage and the ascent stage. The main engine on the descent stage brought the LM down gently on the Moon. The LM landed on four legs with large foot pads.

After exploring the surface, the two astronauts returned to the LM. With its own engine, the ascent stage blasted off from the Moon, using the descent stage as a launch-pad. The ascent of the LM took it back to the CSM, waiting in orbit above. The CSM and LM then docked. The two astronauts crawled through the tunnel linking the spacecraft. The LM was then released to crash into the Moon. The three astronauts returned to Earth in the CSM. Shortly before reentry, the SM dropped away and burned up. The CM was protected by its heat shield from the fiery heat of reentry, which is caused by air resistance. Parachutes opened and the CM splashed down gently in the ocean. Waiting ships retrieved the CM and the crew.

Left The Apollo 9 Lunar Module photographed from the Command/Service Module during the first full test of the Apollo LM in Earth orbit during March 1969.

Right Sequence of diagrams 1 to 10 showing various important stages of an Apollo manned mission to the Moon and back.

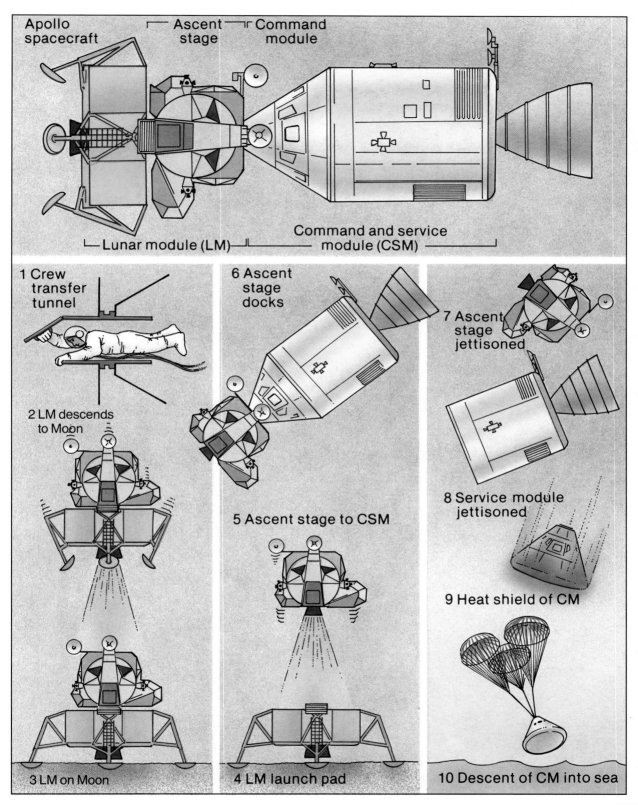

Apollo spacecraft

Ascent stage

Command module

Lunar module (LM)

Command and service module (CSM)

1 Crew transfer tunnel

2 LM descends to Moon

3 LM on Moon

5 Ascent stage to CSM

4 LM launch pad

6 Ascent stage docks

7 Ascent stage jettisoned

8 Service module jettisoned

9 Heat shield of CM

10 Descent of CM into sea

The Space Shuttle

Launching rockets is a very expensive business. They can be used only once. A rocket is completely destroyed in the process of lifting a spacecraft into space. To try to make space travel cheaper, it was decided to make reusable launch vehicles. Both the United States and the USSR have done this. They have built Space Shuttles. A shuttle is cheaper for complicated manned missions, such as repairing or retrieving satellites, or building structures in space. The most expensive part is the Shuttle Orbiter, which can be used over and over again. It carries the crew and cargo into orbit, and returns to Earth, where it can land like a very large glider.

The U.S. Space Shuttle has three main rocket engines. These use fuel from a huge separate tank, called the External Tank, or ET.

At launch the Shuttle rides on the back of the giant ET. This holds liquid hydrogen and oxygen, which are pumped into the Orbiter's engines. The Shuttle blasts off with the help of two giant Solid-fueled Rocket Boosters, or SRBs. They work like giant fireworks rockets. After about two minutes, when the Shuttle is 28 mi (45 km) above the Earth, the boosters separate. They fall back into the ocean and can be used again.

The speed of the Shuttle increases until it reaches a height of about 75 mi (120 km). The fuel in the ET lasts for only about nine minutes, but this is all the time it takes for the Shuttle to get into space. When the main engines shut down, the ET falls away and burns up in the Earth's atmosphere. It is the only part of the Shuttle that cannot be reused. Two other rocket engines on the Shuttle then take over. They are

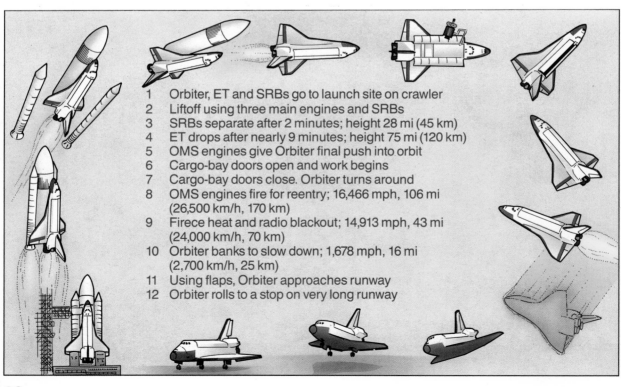

1   Orbiter, ET and SRBs go to launch site on crawler
2   Liftoff using three main engines and SRBs
3   SRBs separate after 2 minutes; height 28 mi (45 km)
4   ET drops after nearly 9 minutes; height 75 mi (120 km)
5   OMS engines give Orbiter final push into orbit
6   Cargo-bay doors open and work begins
7   Cargo-bay doors close. Orbiter turns around
8   OMS engines fire for reentry; 16,466 mph, 106 mi (26,500 km/h, 170 km)
9   Firece heat and radio blackout; 14,913 mph, 43 mi (24,000 km/h, 70 km)
10 Orbiter banks to slow down; 1,678 mph, 16 mi (2,700 km/h, 25 km)
11 Using flaps, Orbiter approaches runway
12 Orbiter rolls to a stop on very long runway

called the Orbital Maneuvering System, or OMS, engines. These give the Shuttle its final boost, and 45 minutes after launch it is in Earth orbit. A second "burn" of the OMS engines puts the Orbiter into a near circular orbit about 186 mi (300 km) above the Earth. The cargo-bay doors are then opened and work begins.

When it is time to return to Earth, the OMS engines are fired forward like retro-rockets. This slows the Orbiter, and it enters the Earth's atmosphere. The surface of the Orbiter is covered with 30,000 special lightweight heat-absorbing tiles. These protect the crew and spacecraft from the fierce heat of reentry. The Orbiter slows down as it reaches the lower part of the atmosphere. Wheels are lowered just before touch-down. It glides in to land on a very long runway and rolls to a stop.

Below The Space Shuttle Challenger, with its cargo-bay doors open, photographed in Earth orbit by astronaut Bruce McCandless, from a distance of 200 ft (60 m), on February 7, 1984.

Above The Soviet Shuttle Buran, Russian for "Snowstorm," sitting piggyback on its giant Energia rocket booster at the launch pad. The first unmanned test flight took place at dawn on November 15, 1988, and was successful. Unlike its U.S. counterpart, the Soviet Shuttle has no main engines of its own. It needs the powerful engines of Energia to launch it into space. The entire Energia/Shuttle combination weighs 2,600 tons. Fuel accounts for over 2,000 tons.

Every space launch is called a mission. U.S. space missions are normally divided into two main parts – launching and flight control. The launch port for the Apollo flights, Skylab space station missions and now the Space Shuttle launches, is the Kennedy Space Center (or KSC for short) in Florida. This has two main areas – the Vehicle Assembly Building (VAB), and the Launch Control Center (LCC). As soon as a spacecraft is launched, control of the flight is handed over to the Mission Control Center (MCC) at the Johnson Spaceflight Center (JSC) just outside Houston in Texas.

The VAB is one of the world's largest buildings. Clouds may gather inside if the doors are left open. Inside, a complete Saturn V rocket for an Apollo flight, or today a Space Shuttle with its Solid Rocket Boosters and External Tank, can be put together on its mobile launch platform. Shuttle Orbiters are first checked out at the Orbiter Processing Facility (OPF) nearby. The launches take place from Launch Complex 39 at the KSC. The completed rocket assembly is taken to the launch pad on a giant tractor.

Above The spectacular U.S. planetary missions of recent years have been controlled from this room at NASA's Jet Propulsion Laboratory in Pasadena, California.

Right Flight director John Cox looks at the large television screens in the front of the mission control room at NASA's Mission Control Center in the Johnson Spaceflight Center, Houston, Texas. On the screens, the current orbit of the Space Shuttle is displayed alongside a close-up view of operations inside the cargo-bay of the Orbiter, during the fifth flight of Columbia in November 1982.

The rocket is checked out again once it is on the launch pad. Several hours before launch the liquid fuels are pumped aboard. A couple of hours before launch, on a manned flight, the astronauts enter their spacecraft. While the countdown is in progress, all spacecraft systems are carefully monitored by computers and teams of scientists. If anything goes wrong, the countdown can be stopped or put on "hold" for a time. Liftoff is delayed until the fault is put right. Then the countdown continues. In the final moments before blast-off, the launch controller can be heard counting off the seconds ". . . 10, 9, 8, 7, 6, 5, 4, 3, 2, 1, zero . . . all engines running . . . liftoff, we have liftoff."

After liftoff, launch control then hands over to the flight directors at mission control. They make decisions on every part of the mission. Each flight director wears a set of headphones and sits in front of a TV screen. Each director has a special job to do. A very large screen in front of the rows of desks shows pictures of the astronauts, the current orbit of the spacecraft and other information, allowing the directors to follow the progress of the mission. All the spacecraft systems are continually checked out by computers on the ground. These "talk" to the computers on the spacecraft. In this way if a problem occurs it can be quickly discovered and soon corrected.

Above The Soviet Space Shuttle bears a startling resemblance to the U.S. version, although it is slightly larger. The body of the Soviet Shuttle is 18 ft (5.6 m) across, compared with the U.S. Shuttle's 17 ft (5.2 m). The OMS engines of the Soviet Shuttle, used to give the final push into Earth orbit, are located at the rear. The Soviet Shuttle is shown here on the runway after its successful first flight in November 1988. During this flight the Shuttle was unmanned and was flown by remote control under the command of flight directors at mission control near Moscow. The Soviet Shuttle can carry a crew of two to four cosmonauts and six passengers. It is covered with over 38,000 heat-absorbing ceramic tiles to protect it on reentry.

Astronauts can live comfortably in space. The spacecraft's cabin is filled with normal air for them to breathe. It is pressurized, so that air pushes on the human body just as it does on Earth. Astronauts can wear normal clothes inside their spacecraft. Life-support systems keep the air at the correct pressure. These clean the air so that it can be used over and over again. Filters remove the poisonous carbon dioxide and the water vapor that the astronauts breathe out, keeping the air smelling fresh. Electricity is also needed. On the U.S. Shuttle, fuel cells make electricity by means of a chemical reaction between hydrogen and oxygen, producing water as a by-product. Until recently, the USSR used solar panels to make electricity from sunlight. Fresh water was brought up from Earth. The latest Russian spacecraft may also use fuel cells.

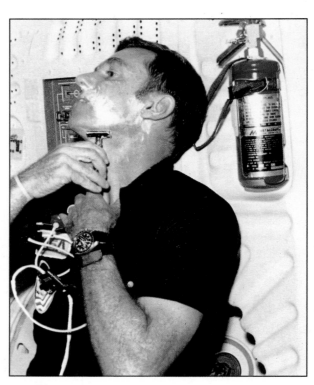

Below Mealtime aboard the Space Shuttle. The metal tray makes for easy meal-preparation.

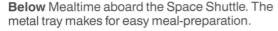

Above On the Space Shuttle Columbia, astronaut Joe Engle shaves using an old-fashioned razor and shaving lather. The lather prevented the cut whiskers from floating around the cabin in the weightless conditions of Earth orbit. This would have caused inconvenience and discomfort to the crew.

Above During crew training, astronaut Rhea Seddon prepares a meal on the Shuttle.

The main difference between living on Earth and in space is the feeling of weightlessness. Everything, including the astronauts, will drift around inside the spacecraft if not fixed down. To get some idea of what it is like to be weightless, look up at the ceiling and imagine there is a book lying there. To get it, you would give a soft push on your chair. You would slowly rise up to the ceiling. Then a soft push against the ceiling would return you to your seat.

Sleeping in space is like "sleeping on a cloud." The body feels no pressure on it from the bed or couch. You could sleep just floating around or get tucked into a lightweight sleeping bag that is taped to the sides of the spacecraft.

You can sleep in any position, even upside down. It all feels the same when you are weightless. Liquids do not flow in weightlessness. So drinks will not stay in cups. Drops of orange juice would just float around inside the spacecraft. Drinks have to be sucked through a plastic straw from a sealed container.

You can eat normal food in space, but space food must be sticky to stay on a spoon or fork. The food is eaten from special packages on a tray, which clips onto the seat or table. Knives, forks and spoons are held by magnets when not in use to stop them floating away. The trays and cutlery are wiped down and reused. Some food is dried and needs hot or cold water added to it.

Once in space, the astronauts have plenty of work to do. To keep fit and well they must get lots of exercise. In space their muscles are not needed to hold them up against the pull of gravity. The astronauts would get weak without exercise, so they use an exercise bicycle or a treadmill to keep fit. While exercising or working, the astronauts stay put by using special handholds, footholds or seat-belts.

Apart from the Shuttle commander and pilot, astronauts called payload specialists and mission specialists go into space. They are often scientists with special skills who carry out experiments or handle payloads. The cargo-bay can hold several small loads and two or three satellites. Satellites are pushed gently out by a special robot manipulator arm. They are then tested in orbit. Lifting does not require any effort in space, but satellites have to be moved with great care. The manipulator arm is worked by remote control from inside the Shuttle. A window looks out on to the cargo-bay. The arm is over 50 ft (15 m) long and is jointed like a human arm.

Below Aboard the Shuttle Discovery, pilot Michael Coats and payload specialist Charles Walker await further calls to duty, while taking a period of rest. The eyeshades help them to sleep.

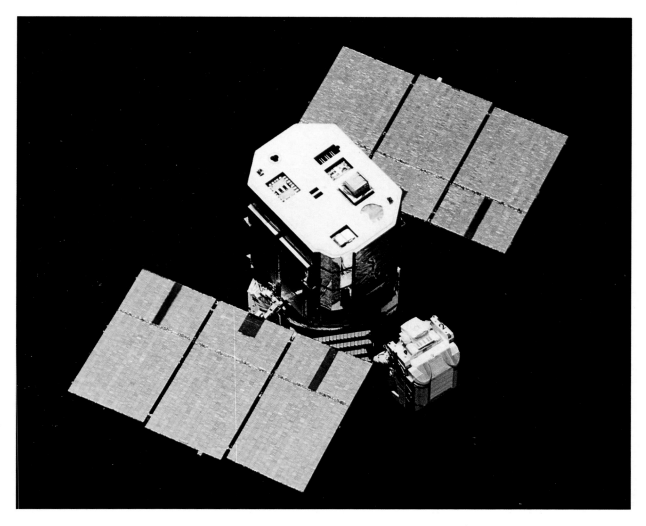

Above Astronaut George Nelson approaches the damaged Solar Maximum Mission satellite in Earth orbit during the fifth flight of the Shuttle Challenger, April 1984.

The Shuttle can be used for repairing or retrieving faulty satellites in low Earth orbits. To repair a satellite is a tricky business. The Shuttle is first brought up very close, and the manipulator arm is extended toward it. Astronauts then have to leave the Shuttle in order to carry out repairs. This is called a spacewalk, or EVA, which stands for Extra-Vehicular Activity. The astronauts may have to fit new parts or replace damaged ones. They often need to hold on to the manipulator arm to keep them from drifting off into space.

The crew enter and leave their spacecraft through an airlock. Spacesuits have to be worn. Each suit has over fifteen layers of plastic and metal to protect the body against the extremes of hot and cold in space. Over the top is a sealed suit with a helmet. These are filled with air at the right pressure. A small life-support system in the backpack supplies air, food and water. An astronaut may use a manned maneuvering unit or MMU, for moving around outside the spacecraft. The MMU is shaped like a chair and is worn as a large backpack. It has 24 small thrusters, which squirt jets of gas like little rockets so the astronauts can move around.

As an important part of their space programs, the United States and the USSR have developed space stations in orbit above the Earth. These space stations were developed so that the Earth and outer space could be more easily observed, and so that scientists could carry out experiments under weightless conditions. A space station also serves as a base where spacecraft can be assembled in readiness for more distant space missions in the future.

The USSR was the first to launch a space station, called Salyut 1, in April 1971. The spacecraft Soyuz 11 docked at one end. Its three-man crew worked aboard the station for 24 days. Sadly, they lost their lives on reentry. The first U.S. space station, called Skylab, was launched nearly two years later.

Skylab was visited by three crews between May 1973 and early 1974. They lived and worked in it for periods of 28, 59 and 84 days. One of Skylab's two huge solar panels and a protective heat shield were damaged during the launch. The first crew worked hard to repair the broken parts. They fitted a sunshade to cool the station.

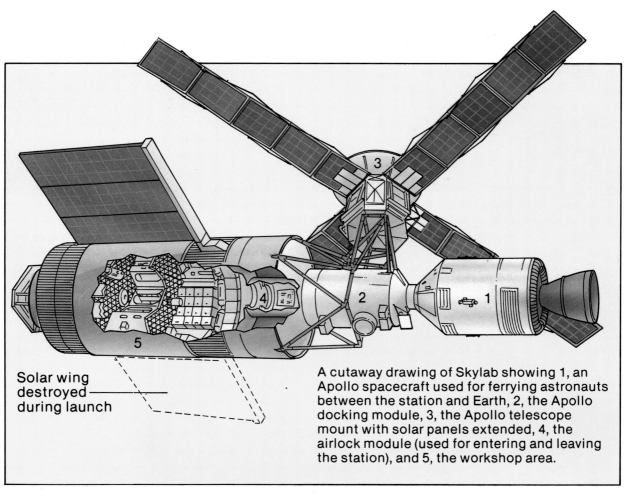

Solar wing destroyed during launch

A cutaway drawing of Skylab showing 1, an Apollo spacecraft used for ferrying astronauts between the station and Earth, 2, the Apollo docking module, 3, the Apollo telescope mount with solar panels extended, 4, the airlock module (used for entering and leaving the station), and 5, the workshop area.

Even though electrical power was reduced, the experiments carried out on Skylab were a great success. Skylab also provided the first opportunity for doctors to study the problems of staying in space for long periods. Weightlessness, cramped conditions, and lack of privacy can cause health problems and make astronauts irritable. Skylab was expected to stay in orbit for ten years. Unfortunately its orbit became too low and it was not possible to boost it higher. In July 1979 Skylab reentered the atmosphere and burned up over the Indian Ocean. Some pieces fell in Australia.

The later Russian Salyut space stations were very successful. The main body of Salyut is 43 by 14 ft (13 × 4.2 m), and weighs 19 tons. A Soyuz spacecraft can dock at either end. Salyut consists of three sections. There is a docking and airlock section, a laboratory and living quarters and a section containing control instruments, attitude control thrusters and the main rocket engine. There is 3,530 cubic ft (100 cubic m) of living and working space for up to six people – about the same as an average-sized living room. Seven Salyut stations have been launched, although Salyut 2 was never manned. All except the most recent, Salyut 7, have now reentered the atmosphere. Teams of cosmonauts, stayed in these stations for several months at a time.

Above This outstanding view of the Skylab space station was taken by the Skylab crew during a "fly around" inspection in the Command Service module. Note that one of the two solar wings on the orbital workshop is missing.

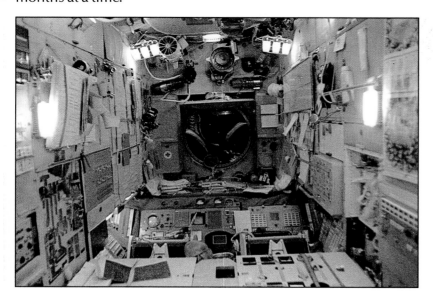

Left The scene aboard the Soviet space station Salyut 6. This station was occupied for a total of 676 days between September 1977 and July 1982, and was home to 16 cosmonaut crews.

The USSR has logged more time in space, by far, than any other nation. Two cosmonauts completed 366 days in orbit just before Christmas 1988. Unlike earlier space stations, Salyuts 6 and 7 could be expanded by the addition of extra "building blocks" or modules. This design is favored both by Soviet engineers and by designers of the future U.S. Space Station. The latest Soviet space station, Mir (Russian for "Peace"), launched in February 1986, can be expanded considerably by the addition of up to six extra modules or spacecraft. In March 1987 a 20-ton laboratory called Kvant was added to Mir.

Crews at present travel up to Mir in Soyuz TM-craft, but they may soon use the Soviet Shuttle. Unmanned supply vehicles carry stores and equipment up to the cosmonauts working there. The present Mir station and its successor Mir-2, with a launch date in the early 1990s, are

Below An artist's impression showing a Space Shuttle Orbiter docked to a manned space station in Earth orbit. There is a connecting tunnel between Shuttle and station.

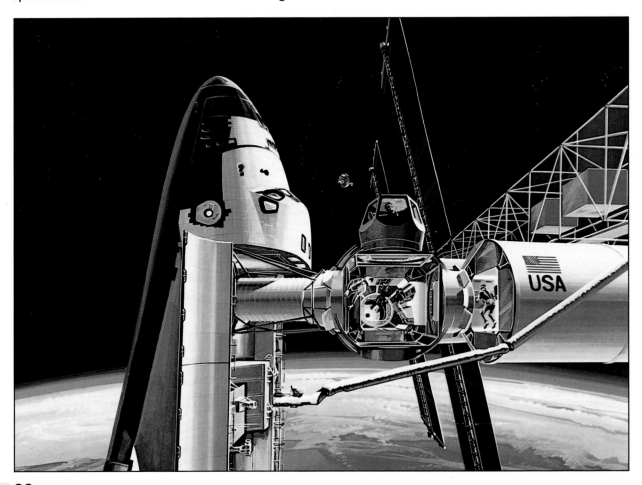

Above A mock-up of a space station of the future. Life-support systems would create a comfortable environment. Handrails enable crew to move about in Zero-gravity.

steps toward the building of huge space station complexes. Such large structures will be built up step-by-step by the addition of new modules. The powerful Energia rocket, which can launch a 100-ton payload into low Earth orbit, will play an important part in the assembly of large Russian space stations over the next ten years.

The United States has planned an international space station called "Freedom." Help from Europe, Japan and Canada is expected. It will be about 395 ft (120 m) long and may cost 20 billion dollars. It will be assembled about 250 mi (400 km) above the Earth in the mid-1990s. Modules carried into orbit by the Space Shuttle will be fitted to a metal framework. There will be living quarters and workshops.

Many things can be made in the weightless conditions in space that are very difficult to make on Earth. In space, alloys made from molten metals stay evenly mixed while they harden. Large, very pure crystals, used in electronic components, can be grown. New medicines for treating the sick may also be produced. One day there may be complete factories in orbit. Some plants may even grow better in space. Already the Russians have set up experiments growing peas and onions in their space stations. Giant space stations may also be used to gather the Sun's rays. The energy would then be beamed down to Earth, where special power stations could store it. This might give us all the fuel we need in the future.

The race to Mars

Of all the planets, Mars is the most likely place for lowly forms of life to exist. Over the next twenty years the race to land humans on Mars will reach its peak. A manned landing is possible by the year 2015. An ambitious program of unmanned missions is already in progress. The USSR may send probes to Mars every two years until the turn of the century. Beginning in 1994, orbiters will map the entire surface.

Balloons will drift around in the thin atmosphere taking detailed photographs by day, descending to test the soil at night. Roving vehicles will wander over the surface examining rocks and soil, taking pictures, watching the weather, and searching for signs of life. By 1996 or 1998, samples collected by a Mars rover might be brought back to Earth orbit by a sample-return probe.

The United States also plans to explore Mars in the 1990s. Due for launch in September 1992, the Mars Observer probe will map the planet in great detail. It may help select landing sites for the next venture, an unmanned rover and sample return mission to be launched in 1998. A soft-lander probe would despatch a rover to travel around for a year collecting samples of rocks and soil. It would then return to the lander and the return probe would blast off, taking the samples up to an orbiter vehicle. The sample container would then be returned to Earth orbit. A major plan to send American astronauts to Mars could well be announced soon. Who gets there first remains to be seen but many people hope to see a truly international mission.

The first manned mission to Mars will probably be a fly-by. Only a few hours would be spent close to Mars. A manned fly-by could pick up samples from return probes, waiting in Mars orbit. By 2002, large rovers driven by astronauts circling overhead in Mars orbit is a possibility. For a manned landing, the Mars lander would be assembled in Earth orbit. About 1,000 tons of payload would have to be lifted into orbit. Unmanned cargo vehicles and possibly the Mars lander would be sent in advance of the main mission. They would carry everything needed for the landing and fuel for the return journey. The manned craft would dock with the cargo vessels before and after landing. The journey would take nine months in each direction, plus a period of a few weeks to several months spent on Mars.

Left In orbit around the planet Mars. This picture shows the smooth, low-lying plain called Argyre in the southern hemisphere of the planet. Three large craters can be seen on the plain, which is encircled by a range of mountains. Layers of atmospheric haze can be seen at the horizon.

Right A full-size mock-up of the Viking Lander spacecraft on the surface of Mars. In the late 1990s, both the Americans and the Russians will send probes to soft-land on the planet. Some will carry roving vehicles that will wander around collecting soil and rock samples. These may even be returned to Earth by a sample-return probe for examination.

Fifty years ago no one would have believed that humans might be living on the Moon or even another planet in the twenty-first century. This is now a very real possibility, and teams of space scientists are already working on the idea. The first stage will be the setting up of large, permanently occupied space stations or huge factories in Earth orbit.

One day there may even be space cities, as first suggested by the Russian rocket pioneer Konstantin Tsiolkovskii. Over 1,000 people might live in such a city. They could produce their own electricity from solar power. All water and many waste products would be recycled to reduce supply needs. Shuttles would bring regular supplies of raw materials and ferry relief crews to and from the Earth.

Colonies on the Moon would be the next step. The Moon's surface is firm enough to support buildings, but it has no atmosphere. Also, it is bitterly cold at night and very hot by day. Supplies for a lunar base would have to come from Earth, which would be very expensive. However, some rare minerals could be mined on the Moon for use on Earth or in space factories in Earth orbit. It is unlikely that work will start on a lunar base before the year 2000. Such a base would probably have a number of inflatable domes. Some would be used as living quarters. Others would serve as workshops. It might even be possible to grow plants inside the lunar base. Large lunar bases making up a colony of several hundred people may be possible by 2025.

Below An artist's impression of a mining operation on the Moon. The lunar soil is scooped up for processing. In the background are the workshops and living quarters.

Above An artist's impression of a large colony on the Moon, where mining operations are taking place. Research has shown that the lunar rocks are rich in various elements, including oxygen, silicon, iron, calcium, aluminum and magnesium.

Mars will almost certainly be the next world to be colonized during the twenty-first century. A colony on the Moon would create a supply base for the more distant planet. Agriculture could develop under pressurized domes on Mars just as on the Moon. By the end of the twenty-first century, Mars could have a population of several thousand. The colonists and all those born on Mars would adapt to the planet's weak gravity. They would find a visit to Earth, with its much stronger gravity, very uncomfortable. Life in domes and underground dwellings on Mars may be all they ever know. The need to wear spacesuits or stay confined within pressurized domes will restrict development on Mars. Perhaps one day someone will find a way of "terraforming" Mars – of giving it an atmosphere like the Earth's. Only then would humans be able to walk unprotected on the surface of Mars.

As yet, the spacecraft launched by the Americans and the Russians have traveled only among the planets. But the first messengers to interstellar space – the space between the stars – are already on their way. The Pioneer and Voyager spacecraft are all heading rather slowly out of the Solar System. It will be thousands of years before they reach other stars. Few people can imagine the huge distances in outer space. The Moon is 240,000 mi (385,000 km) away, and it took astronauts only a few days to get there. The Sun lies 93 million mi (150 million km) distant. The next nearest star beyond the Sun is 24.8 trillion mi (40 trillion km) away. That is over 100 million times more distant than the Moon. Already the numbers are beyond belief, and yet we are only talking about the next nearest star to the Sun.

In spite of the enormous distances to the stars, spacecraft to explore the space beyond the planets could be built today. The technology needed to do so already exists, but a new problem arises – the shortness of the human lifespan. A probe launched by scientists today might take more than one hundred years to reach its destination. The great-grandchildren of the scientists might not be alive to learn the results of the probe.

A plan exists for a spacecraft that could carry a 5-ton payload to a distance of 93 billion mi (150 billion km) in just fifty years. The probe would have to be accelerated to a speed of 62 mi (100 km) per second to reach solar escape velocity. Once in interstellar space it would take accurate measurements of the positions of stars and would send back information to the Earth by laser beam.

Will people ever travel to the stars? Clearly, for human travelers with a typical lifespan of seventy years, new methods are needed. One solution might be to extend the lifespan of the crew by some means not yet discovered, such as "freezing" them for a period of many years. Such forms of travel are beyond existing technologies at present. However, we should remember that in a period of just seventy years we were able to progress in technology from the first powered flight by the Wright brothers to landing men on the Moon. What will happen in the twenty-first century? We shall just have to wait and see.

Below Using the same technology that, in March 1989, took Soviet spacecraft to Mars and its tiny moons, space probes could be built today for traveling toward the stars.
Facing page A first step in this would be a huge space station in Earth orbit.

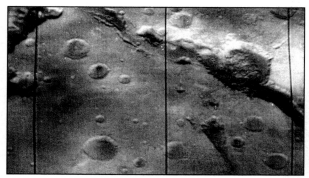

Glossary

Air filter. A device that cleans the air, by removing or filtering out poisonous gases and dust.

Airlock. A sealed chamber with air-tight doors. It allows people to enter or leave a spacecraft without letting the air inside leak into space.

Air pressure. The force exerted by layers of the atmosphere on the layers below and on the ground.

Alloy. A special kind of lightweight but usually strong metal made by mixing together two or more molten metals and then allowing them to cool.

Amplify. To increase the loudness of sounds or the strength of radio signals. The device that does this is called an amplifier.

Aperture. Opening through which light passes in an optical instrument such as a telescope.

Asteroid. One of the many thousands of small, rocky bodies in orbit around the Sun. Most of them lie between Mars and Jupiter.

Astronaut. A person who has been trained to go into space.

Booster rocket. A smaller rocket strapped onto the side of the main rocket engine to give added thrust at blast-off. It is jettisoned when its fuel is used up.

Capsule. The front part of a spacecraft containing the instruments, crew and passengers. The capsule can be separated from the rest of the spacecraft.

Carbon dioxide. A gas found in air. We breathe in oxygen and breathe out carbon dioxide.

Centrifuge. A machine that rotates at very high speed. It is used for training astronauts by subjecting them to very high G-forces.

Comet. A small body in the Solar System, often described as a dirty ice-ball. The only solid part is the nucleus made of ice and rock. A comet may have a long "tail" of dust and gases, which can be seen from Earth.

Command module. The control center and living quarters for the crew of a manned spacecraft.

Coolant. An extremely cold liquid used to cool an instrument to low temperatures.

Cosmonaut. The Russian term for an astronaut.

Countdown. The counting down of the number of seconds to go before a spacecraft is launched.

Dock. To bring together two spacecraft or two parts of a spacecraft.

Eccentric. A word used to describe an orbit that is oval, not circular, where the altitude of the orbiting body varies considerably during each orbit.

Escape velocity. The speed that an object must reach in order to escape from the pull of gravity of a body such as a planet.

Fly-by probe. A type of space probe that passes close to a body in space. A fly-by probe does not land or go into orbit around the target.

Force of gravity. The invisible force that pulls things toward the Earth, or other bodies. Gravity makes objects fall and gives them weight.

Fuel cell. A special device used on a spacecraft to make both electricity and water.

Geostationary orbit. A path around the Earth, at a height of 22,300 mi (35,900 km) above the equator, in which a satellite will always remain above the same point on the Earth's surface.

G-force. The force felt when something is speeding up or slowing down. G-forces throw you forward when a car brakes. The Earth's gravity produces a force of 1G.

Heat shield. A thick layer of special material on the outside of a spacecraft. It protects the spacecraft from the great heat when it reenters the Earth's atmosphere.

Helium. A very stable gas, lighter than air. It is the simplest chemical element after hydrogen. Liquid helium is used as a coolant.

Hydrogen. A colorless, odorless gas, lighter than air. It is the simplest element. Liquid hydrogen is used as a fuel in some rockets.

Infrared. A form of radiation with a wavelength just longer than that of the red light we can see. It can be felt as heat.

Jettison. To throw something away that is no longer needed. To let something fall away.

Laser. A device that amplifies light to produce a very narrow colored beam of light waves, all having exactly the same wavelength.

Life-support system. Equipment that supplies astronauts with air to breathe. It also supplies food and water.

Lift. The force needed to get a spacecraft or aircraft into the air and to keep it from falling. The launch of a rocket is often called liftoff.

Lunar module. The part of the Apollo spacecraft that descended to the surface of the Moon, carrying two crew members.

Manipulator arm. A kind of crane used in space for moving objects, jointed like a human arm.

Manned. A word used to describe a vehicle that contains people. A manned spacecraft contains astronauts.

Manned maneuvering unit (MMU). A piece of equipment used by astronauts to move around in space. It is worn like a large back-pack, and the astronaut sits on it like a chair. It is propelled around by small gas jets.

Manual control. The control or movement of a vehicle or machine by a person.

Multi-stage rocket. A large rocket made up of several separate rockets mounted one on top of the other.

Orbit. The path of one body, such as a planet or satellite, around another body. The Earth moves in orbit around the Sun.

Oxygen. One of the gases found in the Earth's air, and a component of water. Living things breathe in oxygen. Liquid oxygen is also used as a fuel in some rockets.

Pressurize. To alter the air inside the cabin of a spacecraft or inside a spacesuit to make it the same as the air on the ground.

Probe. An unmanned spacecraft sent to examine something at close range.

Reaction. Movement that comes as a result of an action that has happened earlier. When the fuel in a rocket burns, a jet of gases comes out of the back. The reaction is for the rocket to be pushed in the opposite direction to that in which the gases are moving.

Reentry. The moment when a spacecraft comes back into the Earth's atmosphere.

Remote sensing. The use of instruments, such as radar, cameras and heat sensors, to obtain information about the surfaces and atmospheres of distant objects, such as planets, by recording the different types of radiation coming from them.

Retro-rocket. A rocket used for slowing down a spacecraft. It fires in the opposite direction from the main rocket engines.

Robot. A machine that can perform tasks automatically without the help of people, although under their control.

Sample-return probe. A special type of space-probe that soft-lands on another body, such as a planet, scoops up some rocks or soil, and then blasts off again returning them to Earth.

Satellite. A small body in orbit around a larger body in space, such as a planet. The Moon is the Earth's only natural satellite. Many artificial satellites orbit around the Earth. They are used for long-distance communications and for navigation and weather forecasting.

Service module. Part of the Apollo spacecraft, attached to the command module until just before reentry. It contained instruments, fuel cells, food for the crew, a main rocket motor and fuel tanks.

Soft-lander probe. A type of space probe that lands gently on the surface of another body, such as a planet, so that it is undamaged.

Spacesuit. A completely sealed suit of clothing, including a helmet, gloves and shoes.

Thrust. The force that drives a rocket or a spacecraft forward and upward.

Thruster. A small gas jet that works like a tiny rocket. As the gas rushes out, the thruster pushes in the opposite direction.

Ultraviolet. A form of radiation with a wavelength just shorter than that of the violet light we can see. Ultraviolet rays cause sunburn.

Unmanned. A word used to describe a vehicle that does not contain any people.

Vacuum. An empty space that contains no air of any kind or other matter in it.

X-ray. A form of highly penetrating radiation, which has a wavelength shorter than that of ultra-violet radiation, invisible to the human eye.

Further reading

Apfel, Nicia H., *Space Law.* (Franklin Watts, 1988). *Space Station.* (Franklin Watts, 1987).

Hawkes, Nigel, *Space Shuttles: A New Era?* (Franklin Watts, 1989).

Herda, D. J., *Research Satellites.* (Franklin Watts, 1987).

Kerrod, Robin, *See Inside a Space Station.* (Warwick, 1988).

Lambert, Mark, *Transportation in the Future.* (Bookwright, 1986).

Lampton, Christopher, *Rocketry: From Goddard to Space Travel.* (Franklin Watts, 1988).

Space Sciences. (Franklin Watts, 1983). *The Space Telescope.* (Franklin Watts, 1987). *Star Wars,* (Franklin Watts, 1987).

Sandak, Cass R., *The World of Space.* (Franklin Watts, 1989).

Vbrova, Zuza, *Space and Astronomy.* (Gloucester, 1989).

Vogt, Gregory, *Space Explorers.* (Franklin Watts, 1989). *Space Laboratories.* (Franklin Watts, 1989). *Space Satellites.* (Franklin Watts, 1988). *Spaceships.* (Franklin Watts, 1989).

Picture Acknowledgments

The publishers would like to thank The Research House (TRH) for obtaining and supplying the photographs for this book, and also the following for allowing their photographs to be reproduced:
Grumman Aircraft 37; Hughes Aircraft 5, 11, 12 (above); Martin Marietta 21; National Aeronautics and Space Administration (NASA) 4, 6, 7, 13, 14 (below), 15, 16, 17 (below), 22, 23, 24, 27 (below), 28 (both), 30 (both), 31, 32, 33, 35 (above), 36, 38, 39, 40, 41, 43; Novosti Press Agency 8, 17 (above), 27 (above), 29, 35 (below), 42 (both); TRH 10 (above).
Artwork by Nick Hawken.

Index